D1136145

SHIATSU WITH HORSES

CONTENTS

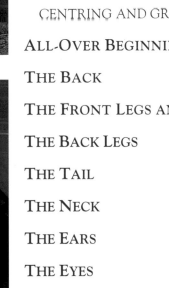

Caution Pamela Hannay is a very experienced shiatsu practitioner. Novice practitioners should take all necessary safety precautions when working in close contact with horses. It is advisable to begin working with an animal known to have a calm, kind temperament!

INTRODUCTION

THE BENEFITS OF TREATMENT

Giving shiatsu treatments to your horse will help you to get to know him and to communicate with him. Communication by touch is extremely powerful and this sensitive and educated way of touching may enhance an already long-standing friendship, as well as help form a new one. Because you will literally be more in touch with your horse's body, you will gain an understanding that will alert you to problems before they get too serious, and you will be better able to assist your vet in determining the causes of certain ailments. Muscular aches and pains associated with training will be released more quickly with regular sessions. In general, horses who receive regular shiatsu treatments are happier, more balanced physically and mentally and recover more quickly from trauma. They understand their own bodies better and their concentration may improve. The deep relaxation they experience during and after a session is obvious and heartwarming. You will feel the benefits in yourself as your body becomes more flexible, and your focus more centred.

LENGTH OF EACH SESSION

A full body session may take about an hour, although sometimes you may do a mini session of just the ears and face, or the feet, or the back, that will take 15 minutes or so. If your horse has a short attention span, finish the session before he is ready to be finished and leave him wanting a bit more, rather than you losing his attention first. Sometimes you may want to take a break during the session and go for a walk together if he becomes fidgety, then resume the

shiatsu session. Always stay sensitive to his needs as you work. Most horses will benefit from weekly sessions but a mini session before and after you ride is ideal. Vary your procedure from time to time so neither of you becomes bored.

AFTER THE SESSION

Leave him in his stable for about five minutes to quietly enjoy some peaceful relaxation time, then turn him out for a while. You may see him run and buck, roll, or he may seem to meditate on some distant object while enjoying the sensations in his body. Observe him carefully as he moves and expresses himself. Do not ride him for at least 15 minutes. He may decide to stand near you and say thank you.

YOUR PREPARATION

Remove your watch and rings. Wear protective footwear and clothing that allows for freedom of movement. If working in the horse's stable, let people in the area know what you are doing so that noise may be kept to a minimum.

CENTRING AND GREETING

Take a few deep breaths and let go of your thoughts, worries, and expectations. Be in the moment, with your horse and yourself.

WHAT NOT TO TREAT

- Areas of broken skin – open wounds – areas that have been stitched or areas near these locations – inflamed joints where heat can be felt – broken bones.
- Always consult your vet if your horse is injured or displaying extreme personality changes.

This is your time together, although other friendly animals will want to be near the peaceful atmosphere of the shiatsu session. If you know your horse very well, kneel nearby so that he lowers his head to you. If you do not know him that well, stand near his head quietly for a moment and let him hear your calm soft breathing. Always wait for his acknowledgement of you and permission to begin; the

horse notices you, comes over to you and makes some sort of gentle accepting contact, like sniffing you or blowing softly, nuzzling and investigating. This is a sign that he is ready to be touched, which I feel is permission to begin. He may also give you a nudge. Try to begin and finish the session the same way each time so he understands what is expected of him, which is to stand quietly and enjoy himself. Keep your breathing deep but not exaggerated as you work. Enjoy this precious time of communication together, which will surely deepen your relationship.

ALL-OVER BEGINNING TOUCH

Allow your hands to flow smoothly by moving your body like a soft reed being bent by the breeze. The movement is initiated from the centre of your body in your lower abdomen. Your knees will bend as you cover the lower portions of his body. Begin this sweeping, stroking touch a few inches from the poll, progressing rearward and downward, moving your hands alternately, in long movements. The pressure is firm but extremely gentle.

continues ▶

PURPOSE OF THE ALL-OVER BEGINNING TOUCH

This first technique will make your horse aware of himself and his physical boundaries. It will tell him that his bodywork session is about to begin and will stimulate his skin and the areas just underneath. It will quickly give you the opportunity to assess his condition regarding body temperature variation, muscle tightness and relaxation level. With experience, you will learn a great deal in terms of evaluating his overall condition by using this as an opening technique.

THE BACK

PALMING THE BLADDER MERIDIAN

Drape your left hand across the withers as shown, or an inch or so to either side. Keeping full contact through to the tips of the fingers, allow your palm to find its place, molding to the contours of his body. Let it sink in a bit without actually pressing. Your right hand is alongside the left, also draped across his back and in complete contact through the fingertips. Lean into the right hand a little. At the moment, your left hand is your **supporting hand** and your right hand is your **working hand**. Your left hand will stay at the withers until your working hand is about halfway down his back, or until your hands feel 'out of touch' with each other. Then, move your supporting hand to an area further along his back or close to the location of your working hand.

the next position, a few inches along, or the distance of the width of your hand, then the supporting hand sinks in, immediately followed by the working hand. Proceed in this way toward the dock of the tail.

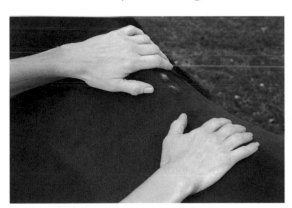

Procedure The supporting hand sinks in, then the working hand sinks in, then hold both hands with the same pressure for several seconds. Begin to gradually release pressure in both hands in preparation for the next location of your working hand. The supporting hand pressure releases only halfway while the working hand prepares to contact its next location. Place your working hand in

Moving from your centre Moving from your centre will keep your body relaxed, especially your shoulders, if you are working on a tall horse. Staying relaxed will keep you from becoming tired as you work. Also, if your body is tension free, you will become more sensitive to the delicate nuances of his body.

Breathing As you lean towards him to sink into his back with your palms, try doing so on your exhalation, even if you are staying on a particular location for more than one breath's length of time. Your breathing should always be slow and relaxed and feel as if it is coming from below your navel. Proper breathing, moving from your centre and using both hands as described will enable you to gain as much benefit from this work as your horse does.

FINGERTIP PRESSURE

Use your supporting hand in the way previously described. With your working hand, make a unit of your fingertips by curving your hand slightly and holding your fingers alongside one another. Place them in the same channel as you did previously with your palm (bladder meridian). Sink in with your supporting palm, then with the working hand's fingertips and hold for a few seconds. The sinking in as well as the release is gradual and slow. Never rush these techniques.

(*See photos opposite*)

PALMING AND FINGERTIP TECHNIQUES FOR THE BACK

1. The purpose of the supporting hand: if your working hand touches a sensitive area on the horse's back, the prior contact of the supporting hand will help distract and disperse the pain and help him to feel comfortable, stabilized and supported. It will act as a monitor to detect areas of soreness in your working hand. Your two hands will be in communication with each other.

2. Your angle of penetration should be vertical to the area you are touching. Take care that your horse does not feel he is being pushed over and has to support his body with his far side legs each time you press.

3. Your entire body should feel relaxed. Your knees should be slightly bent and your feet about hip width apart. The foot that is opposite your working hand should be slightly behind to keep you in a balanced position, for example, if your working hand is the left hand, your right foot should be placed slightly behind you. Your shoulders and arms are relaxed so that all the inward pressure can be created by leaning your body from your centre. Your entire body reflects a roundness, and your face has a pleasant relaxed expression.

4. Keep your elbow, wrist and hand rounded softly so your own energy may flow while you stay relaxed as you work. The contact of your fingertips may feel more specific to your horse, especially in sensitive areas, so be especially mindful of his reactions. If you have time, after practising the fingertip technique on both sides, do the palming again. You may notice that any previously sensitive or tight areas have released, relaxed and feel more balanced. Always observe your horse's reactions as you work. Working in this way will deepen the two-way communication between you.

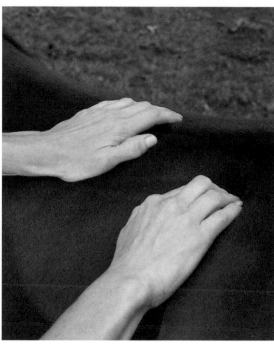

HOW MUCH PRESSURE?

This depends on the individual horse. Any pressure, deep or light, should be applied gradually and released gradually. For example, on a scale of 1–10, if you are using pressure-level 7, take at least three seconds to build to the final amount of pressure, then hold for a few (5–10) seconds, then take another three or so seconds to withdraw your pressure before moving on. Let each location you touch 'tell' you how long to stay and how much pressure to use. In areas where you feel you are able to sink in a bit, you will stay relatively longer. These areas may give you the impression that they are pulling you in. Other areas, those of tension and sensitivity, may give you the impression of pushing you away. These are areas that should be touched more briefly and lightly because they may be painful. By staying longer in the receptive areas, the energy movement created may greatly dissipate the pain in the tense tight places.

ADVICE FOR WORKING ON THE BACK

Please do not worry about being precise in your location of the bladder meridian immediately. As you develop your technique and relax your body, you will become increasingly able to feel the meridian and its energy flowing. Focus on your breathing, relaxation, moving from your centre, and concentrating on your horse.

AUTHOR'S TIP

Always try to begin on what may be the less sensitive side first. You may palm, then finger-tip-work one side, then the other, or palm each side first, then work each side with the fingertips. You may repeat each of these techniques up to three times on each side.

THE FRONT LEGS AND SHOULDERS

LEG JIGGLE

Squat in front and to the side of the horse's front leg facing toward his rear. Place your overlapped hands behind his upper leg. Bounce it lightly and loosely toward you, causing the muscles surrounding the shoulder to jiggle and perhaps even undulate. Observe the effect as you do this 5–10 times. You may use this technique before and after the shoulder rotation, as it will act as a monitor of the rotations' effect. Be patient if he thinks you want him to lift his leg the first few times.

FRONT LEG AND SHOULDER ROTATIONS

This technique will help make his shoulders more supple, as well as help you understand his normal range of motion and joint condition. It will keep the horse aware of himself too, as you practise these gentle movements.

First, lift the leg by sliding your hand nearest the horse down his leg and leaning against him lightly. When he lifts his foot off the ground, immediately catch it under the hoof with your free hand. Position your other hand under his knee and support him with his lower leg parallel to the ground and directly underneath his shoulder. Take a soft stance with your knees slightly bent. Begin to move your body in a circular movement, taking his leg with you. This movement, which starts with a small rotation, will have a pleasant effect upon his shoulder, relaxing its muscles and moving any blocked energy there. The first few circles should only be about six inches in diameter. Gradually build the size of this rotation to about 12 inches, depending upon the size of your horse. Rotate in both directions from three up to eight or 10 times. You may notice that one of the directions feels more natural for him than the other. Lower his leg to the ground by holding one hand on each side of his hoof, bending your knees and placing his foot quietly down. Repeat with the other foreleg.

JIGGLE AND ROTATE

Repeat this sequence of jiggle, rotation, jiggle, on each side, beginning with his 'easier' side, before you progress to the next technique.

FOOT ROTATIONS

Pick up the first leg and position it across your bent leg, near your knee. The concave portion of his fetlock joint should fit over the convex portion of your leg, which is going a bit uphill. Make certain he feels secure with his leg positioned comfortably underneath his shoulder and his lower leg parallel to the ground. Hold his foot above the hoof with a secure supporting hand, and his toe with the other hand. Moving from your centre, slowly rotate his foot a few times in each direction, exploring its range of motion. Do not force the movement or try to increase it beyond its normal range.

RAISED LEG SWING

While you still have his foot off the ground, place one hand underneath his hoof and the other across the front of his knee. Using only the hand that is on his knee, swing his leg toward and away from you, creating a loose free movement in his shoulder. Look up and observe the movement in his shoulder. Swing back and forth several times without actually grabbing his knee. The movement should come from your body, which is moving with his shoulder. Reduce the movement gradually and then replace his foot on the ground using your hands on each side of his hoof. Repeat the sequence of foot rotation and raised leg swing once with each foreleg before continuing to the full leg stretch.

FULL LEG STRETCH

The previously explained techniques will have prepared your horse for this stretching technique. Go to the first leg and lift it into the rotation position. Rotate it a few times and step rearward as you position your hands behind his knee and fetlock. Shift your weight into your rear leg and hold without pulling or forcing. His leg should be directly in front of his shoulder and in alignment with it. Never force this stretch. If your horse wants more of a stretch, he will lean rearward and create it himself. You may hold him in this position for 5–10 seconds. Replace the leg then repeat this stretch on his other side. Note that each side may have a different degree of elasticity. Carefully observe his reactions to your technique.

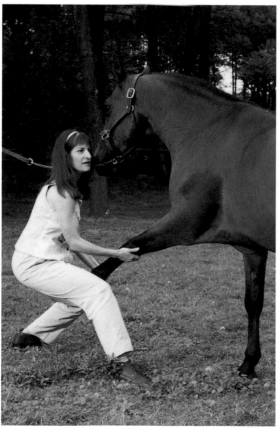

PROPER REPLACEMENT OF THE LEG

To return his leg to the ground, shift your weight to your forward leg, then step forward as you bend his leg. Then, hold both sides of his hoof and lower your body and return his foot to the ground.

SMOOTH PROGRESSION

Always proceed smoothly from one technique to the next, and keep your hands on him as you make the transition from one side to the other. Sometimes you may want to walk him after completing one or two techniques in order to let him observe any newly felt freedom of movement. Speak to him softly and praise him when he understands how to work with you to achieve harmony in your shiatsu session.

Also, note that his front end may now feel much more enlivened and comfortable than his rear end; if you have taken a walking break, he may look and move as if he is aware of that fact as well.

THE BACK LEGS

LEG SWING

Encourage your horse to rest his leg on his toe. Squat, facing toward his leg. Place one hand on or just above the hock joint, the other hand in front of his leg for support. Using his hock as a sort of lever, gently swing his leg to and fro several times. This loose and free swinging motion will relax his quarters and prepare him for leg rotations and stretches.

BACK FOOT ROTATIONS

Lift his leg and let it rest in your hands, one of which is under his fetlock joint, and the other is holding the tip of his hoof. Take a wide stance with bent knees. You may need to lean your upper arm on your knee for your support. While holding his leg in a stable position, rotate his hoof slowly two or three times. Try to isolate only this joint and rotate in each direction. Then, repeat with the other leg.

BACK LEG
ROTATIONS AND STRETCHES

Holding the horse's leg under his fetlock joint and under his hoof, and maintaining your wide stance position, move your body in a small circular motion, taking his leg with you. His lower leg is resting in your hands. The first few rotations are done with his leg directly under his hip, with circles only about 10 inches in diameter. Next, move his leg slightly rearward, still rotating. Continue this rearward movement, while rotating his leg, by moving your body until his leg is 12–16 inches directly behind him. If he continues to relax and release his leg

comfortably to you, **stop rotating**, then, lean your body forward slowly by continuing to shift your weight into your front leg. This stretch should be fairly easy for both of you if he is happy and you are not forcing the stretch.

TO FINISH THE STRETCH AND REPLACE THE LEG

You will learn to sense when he has had enough. Just before this point, slowly begin to shift your weight into your rear leg, thereby returning his leg to a neutral position with his toe on the ground. The stretch may be held for several seconds. You may then do the leg swing again.

FORWARD STRETCH

As you become proficient with shifting your weight while holding his leg, try to stretch his leg forward as a continuous follow-on to the rearward stretch. As you carry the leg from the rearward stretch position, adjust your hand positions so that each hand wraps around the rear of his leg, from the inside and outside of the leg. You will now be shifting your weight as you step backwards while lowering yourself downward into a crouched position alongside his front leg. His rear hoof should be aimed toward his front hoof, not to the inside or to the outside. Do not bounce or pull his leg. Observe the stretch as you hold it for a few seconds. If he seems in the least unsure, speak to him encouragingly and return his leg to the ground under his hip.

Always return his hoof to the ground by lowering yourself with it, holding the sides of his hoof with two hands. If desired, you may repeat the rearward stretch again. After working on both rear legs, take a moment to rest and compliment him (and yourself). You may wish to walk him for a few minutes before continuing.

DEVELOPING SENSITIVITY

As you develop your sensitivity during these techniques, try to hold him just under his maximum stretch capacity. If he wants to stretch more, he may lean forward. Be patient with him, and yourself, so that, in time, these movements become like a graceful dance between you.

THE TAIL

TAIL MOVEMENT AND MANIPULATION

By now, your horse should be extremely relaxed and happy. Stand behind him and gently take hold of his tail, stroking the hair gently downward, with your hands underneath the tail. Then, walk to each side of his body, taking the tail with you, and draping it across his quarters on each side for a few seconds. Keep it fairly low on the hindquarters, without actually pulling. Notice if the sides feel different from each other in terms of flexibility as you move his tail from side to side.

Then, rotate each vertebra by holding securely with the upper hand from underneath, with the other hand moving the tail in small circles in each direction. Work your way down the tail by keeping your hands fairly close together and moving slowly. The upper and middle sections may move very easily.

BE OBSERVANT

Continuously observe his ears and attitude toward this technique. If you feel at all uncertain of his reactions, discontinue this tail sequence for now.

Next, place one hand under and one hand over his tail. The underneath hand, which is in the higher position, raises the tail slightly upward. Almost immediately the other hand gently draws the tail downward. Proceed in this way toward the end of his tail bones or until you feel there is no more movement.

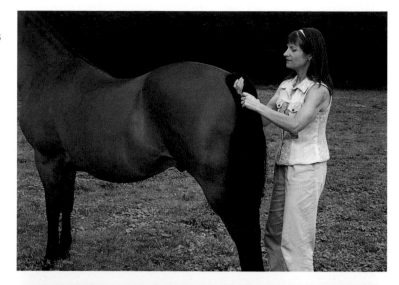

TAIL STRETCHING

To stretch the tail, and also the entire spine, hold the tail from underneath, with separated hands, and begin to lean your body rearward. Do not pull, just lean. He should straighten his head and then lean into his stretch. Hold this position for several seconds or as long as he seems to be enjoying himself.

To release the stretch, gradually shift your weight into your forward leg by pulling yourself toward him slowly. Walk to his head and ask him how it feels to have a tail.

THE NECK

ROCKING THE NECK

Place your hands over the crest of the horse's neck. Lean forward and backward, moving your entire body to rock his neck from side to side. This movement will cause his head to tilt back and forth loosely and freely. If he has any objection, decrease the movement or change the location of your hands. This is a free-swinging energetic movement for both of you. Rock for about 10 seconds.

PALMING THE NECK

Place your palm on his neck, a few inches from the poll, halfway between its upper and lower portion, i.e. on a line directly along the centre of his neck. Your supporting hand is on the other side of his neck, in a similar location. Lean into your working palm, but keep his neck from moving away from you by holding, not pressing, with your supporting palm. Continue down toward his shoulder in increments of a few inches, moving your supporting palm each time your working hand moves.

Next, beginning slightly away from the poll, work on the upper portion of his neck, maintaining your vertical pressure relative to

the area you are touching. Your supporting hand is under the large muscle on the bottom half of the opposite side of his neck, pressing upward to support the downward pressure of your working hand. Continue working the top line toward his shoulder.

Then, work the area under the muscle on the same side, allowing your working palm to mold to the contours of his neck. Your supporting hand on the opposite side is holding along the top portion of his neck, i.e. the ridge under his mane, pressing slightly downward to support your working hand.

Repeat on the other side of the neck.

MOVING THE NECK

Place your palm in the area of the centre line, a few inches from the poll. Your supporting hand is placed across the horse's face, about halfway from the eyes to the mouth. Lean into his neck a little, hold, and bring his head an inch or two toward you, keeping his head from tilting or twisting. Return his head to its neutral position as you release the pressure in your working hand. Continue toward his shoulder, bringing his head toward you and then returning it to its neutral position with each incremental position of your working hand. It may help to keep eye contact with him during this exercise and to speak to him encouragingly.

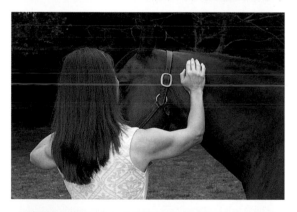

GRADUAL PRESSURE AND RELEASE

Work on the more flexible side of the horse's neck, if he has one. The inward pressure of your working hand is gradual, as is the release. Hold each area for a few seconds. If he doesn't accept the neck work, go back to a technique he enjoys.

THE EARS

Place your hand against the horse's head with your index finger in front of the ear, and three fingers behind. Do not squeeze, rather, mold your hand to the contours of his head at the base of his ear. Hold him across the nose softly with your other hand. Then, rotate the ear by moving the skin at its base. The pressure of your working hand should be firm. Rotate several times in each direction.

Using the same finger/thumb method , walk up the ear, alternating hands, while you traction the ear slightly toward you. Go slowly and do not pull.

Then, walk the fingertips up the ear while tractioning it slightly rearward, holding it away until you reach the tip.

Lastly, traction the ear forward as you alternately walk your fingers toward the tip.

You may finish with another rotation as described in the first ear technique. Repeat with the other ear.

Next, apply fingertip pressure up the outside edges of the ear by placing your thumbs on the inside edges and your fingertips on the outside edges of the ear. Walk up the ear toward the tip with your fingertips. Take care not to apply your thumbs too far inside, as he may be sensitive or ticklish there.

THE EYES

Cup your hand and lean it lightly against his head above his eye. Apply your thumb to the upper socket bone, pressing upward so as not to slip. Work your way along the upper socket bone, starting at the inner corner and progressing outward.

Using the three middle fingertips, work the under-eye area, pressing gently downward. Begin at the inner corner and proceed toward the outer corner. At the outer corner, work outward for an inch or two.

Repeat with the other eye.

THE FACE

Beginning at the inner corner of his eye, and using your fingertips as a unit, work downward toward his nose, along the route of the tear duct. Work at very small intervals all the way to his nostrils. Repeat on the other side.

THE CHEEK

Cup your hand under the large cheek muscle, letting it rest in your hand. Move your hand at regular intervals, pressing upward, to relax his cheek and jaw. Repeat with the other cheek.

THE MOUTH

Hold the horse across the nose from underneath. Using the web of your hand, (between the thumb and forefinger) pull his lower lip downward, and press the web of your hand along the gum line, moulding your hand to its contours. Then, slide your hand back and forth a few times.

Next, do the upper gum line. If his mouth seems dry, you may dip your hand in some water to moisten it. Then, give him a moment to assimilate what is perhaps a very new sensation.

Then, slide your thumb inside his mouth, keeping it as close as possible to the inside of his cheek. Reach up a bit, then, draw your hand downward, and out of his mouth after you have completed this movement.

JAWS!

Take care to avoid contact with his teeth. He should be wearing a loose headcollar (halter) or none at all, to avoid restriction of your hand and to allow for yawning space.

To finish your session, repeat the all-over stroking you used at the beginning. Stand quietly with your horse a moment or two, and leave him to enjoy the effects of shiatsu.

FOALS AND YOUNG HORSES

Each new day in a foal's life brings a wealth of lessons. Many of these lessons are taught by mother, some are learned by exploring his territory. The rate of growth is fast. You see the baby growing before your eyes. Keep the bond between you and the mother strong by giving her shiatsu during gestation as well as after the foal is born. This will help her stay well as the new demands of motherhood tax her energy.

Create an indelible bond between you and your foal immediately by voice and touch. Try some simple techniques with gentle pressure on a regular basis. Your session may last only a moment, so respond to whatever area the baby presents. Be ready to work on the move. Mother may demand some attention as well. Stay in touch with both their bodies as they change, and most of all, have fun!

To Jacqueline Cook for her enthusiastic promotion of this beautiful work in the UK.

ACKNOWLEDGEMENTS

My thanks to Joy Spanier for my model, Trittons Rothchild (Morgan horse), to Jacqueline Cook and Gee Bee, born 29th May, 1998 (dam: Beebob – New Forest x Thoroughbred; sire: Golden Heights – registered Thoroughbred) and to Peter Cook for the photographs on page 23.

British Library Cataloguing-in-Publication Data.
A catalogue record for this book is available from the British Library

© J. A. Allen
First published in Great Britain 1999
Reprinted 2006

ISBN-10: 0-85131-761-8
ISBN-13: 978-0-85131-761-8

J.A. Allen
Clerkenwell House
Clerkenwell Green
London EC1R 0HT

J.A Allen is an imprint of Robert Hale Limited

Design and Typesetting by Paul Saunders
Series editor Jane Lake
Colour processing by Tenon & Polert Colour Processing Ltd., Hong Kong
Printed in China by Midas Printing International Limited